PIANO • VOCAL • GUITAR

TOP CHRISTIAN HITS OF 2010-2011

ISBN 978-1-61780-316-1

7777 W. Bluemound Rd. P.O. Box 13819 Milwaukee, WI 53213

Visit Hal Leonard Online at
www.halleonard.com

BEAUTIFUL

Words and Music by MERCYME,
DANIEL MUCKALA and BROWN BANNISTER

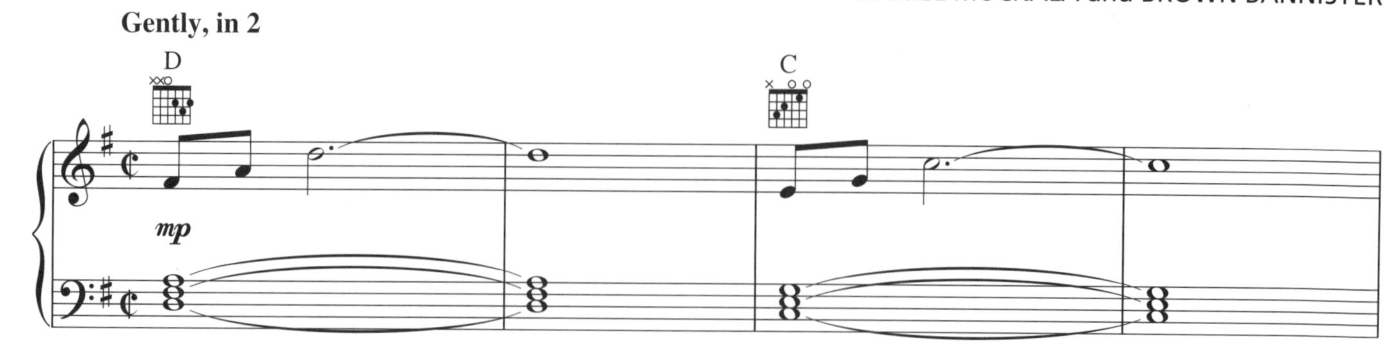

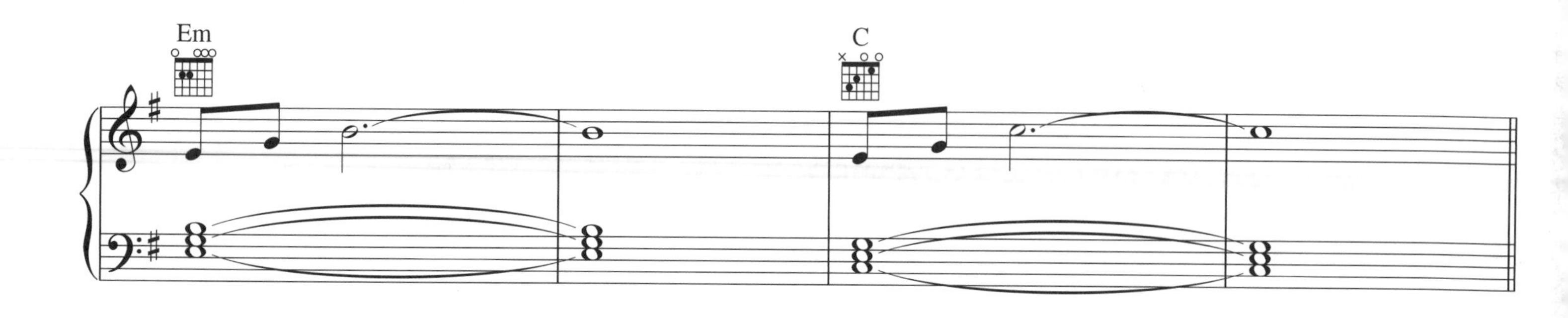

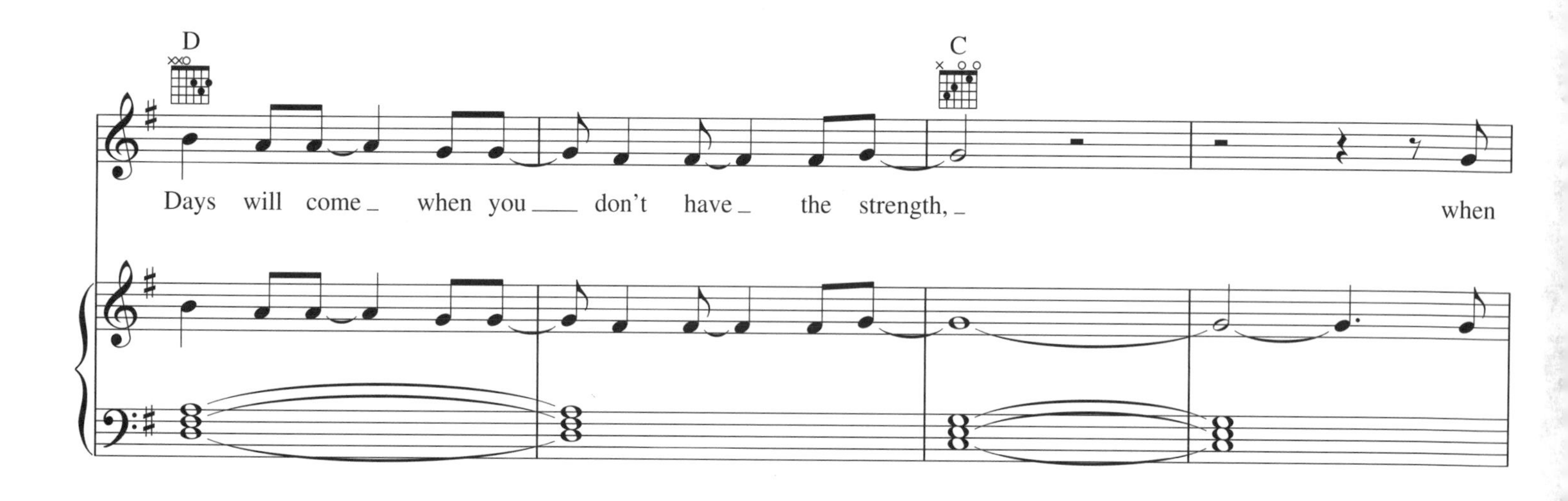

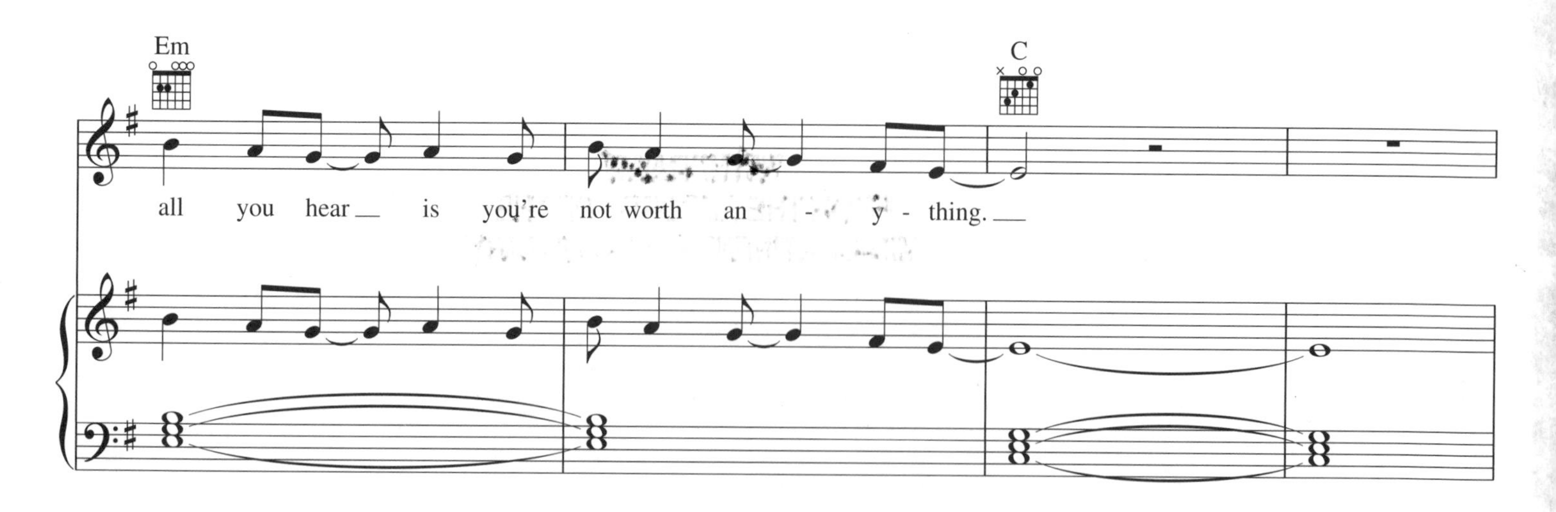

D
C
Won-d'ring if you ev - er could be loved,
and if they tru -
Em
C
- ly saw your heart, they'd see too much.
You're beau - ti - ful,
G
C
you're beau - ti - ful.
You are made
Em
C
for so much more than all of this.
You're beau - ti - ful,

G
C
you're beau - ti - ful,
you are treas -
Em
C
- ured, you are sa - cred, you are His.
You're beau - ti - ful.
G
C
mf
Em
C
I'm

D
C
pray - ing that you have the heart to fight,
Em
'cause you are more than what is hurt - ing you to - night.
C
D
For all the lies you've held
C
in - side so long,
and they are noth -

Em
C
- ing in the shad - ow of the cross.
G
You're beau - ti - ful,
you're beau - ti - ful.
C
Em
You are made for so much more
C
than all of this.
You're beau - ti - ful,

G
C
you're beau - ti - ful.
Em
You are treas - ured, you are sa - cred, you are
C
D
His.
You're beau - ti - ful.
Be - fore you ev -
C
- er took a breath, long be - fore the world be - gan,

D
C
of all the won - ders He pos - sessed, there was one
D
more pre - cious. Of all the earth and skies a - bove,
C
D
you're the one He mad - ly loves, e -
C
nough to die.

G
C
You're beau - ti - ful,
mp
Em
you're beau - ti - ful
in His
C
eyes.
G
D
C

D
Em
Bm
C
G
Bm
You're beau - ti - ful.
mf
C
You were meant
for so much more than all of this.
Em
Bm
C

G
Bm
You're beau - ti - ful.
C
1
Em
Bm
You are treas - ured, you are sa - cred, you are His.
C
You're beau - ti - ful.
2
Em
D
C
- ured, you are sa - cred, you are His.
rit.

BEFORE THE MORNING

Words and Music by JOSH WILSON
and BEN GLOVER

A
Dsus2
May - be there are things you can't see, and all those things are hap -
F♯m
Dsus2
Esus
- pen - ing to bring a bet - ter end - ing. Some - day, some - how you'll
Dsus2
Esus
A
E/G♯
see, you'll see. Would you dare, would you dare to be - lieve
mf
F♯m7
D
that you still have a rea - son to sing? 'Cause the pain that you've been feel - ing,

E
A
E/G♯
it can't com-pare to the joy that's com-ing.
So hold on, you got-ta wait for the light,
F♯m7
D
To Coda
press on and just fight the good fight.
'Cause the pain that you've been feel - ing,
E
A
D
Esus
E
it's just the dark be-fore the morn-ing.
A
D/A
My friend, you know how this all ends, and you know where you're go -

F♯m
D
E
- ing, you just don't know how you'll get ___ there. So say a prayer ___ and hold ___
A
D/A
___ on, 'cause there's good for those ___ who love ___ God. But life is not a snap -
F♯m
D
E
D.S. al Coda
- shot; it might take a lit - tle time, ___ but you'll see the big - ger pic - ture.
CODA
E
A
it's just the dark be - fore the morn - ing. ___ Yeah, ___ yeah, ___

D
F♯m7
before the morning.
Yeah,
yeah.
D
E
Once you feel the weight
A/C♯
D
E
of glory,
all your pain will fade
A/C♯
D
E
to memory.
Once you feel the weight

A/C♯
D
E
of glo - ry,
all your pain will fade
A/C♯
D
to mem - o - ry, mem - o - ry, mem - or - y, yeah.
E
A
E/G♯
Would you dare, would you dare to be - lieve
F♯m7
A7/C♯
D
that you still got a rea - son to sing?
'Cause the pain that you've been feel - ing,

E
A
E/G♯
it can't com-pare to the joy that's com-ing.
Would you dare, would you dare to be - lieve
F♯m7
D
that you still got a rea - son to sing?
'Cause the pain that you've been feel - ing,
E
A
A/G♯
F♯m7
E
it can't com-pare to the joy that's com-ing.
Come on, you got - ta wait for the light,
F♯m7
F♯m7/E
F♯m7/C♯
A
D
press on and just fight the good fight.
'Cause the pain that you've been feel - ing,

E
Bm7
A/C♯
it's just the hurt be-fore the heal-ing.
Oh, the pain that you've been feel-ing,
D
E
it's just the dark
be-fore the morn-ing,
A
D
be-fore the morn-ing.
F♯m7
D
Esus
Yeah,
yeah,
be-fore the morn-ing.

EVERYTHING I NEED

Words and Music by JON MICAH SUMRALL
and DAVE LUBBEN

B♭/F
E♭(add2)
6fr
I can - not climb, You car - ry me.
Je - sus,
Cm7
3fr
car - ry me.
B♭
You are
f
F
Gm7
E♭
3fr
B♭
F
Gm7
strength in my weak - ness, and You are the ref - uge I seek.
B♭
F
Gm7
You are ev - 'ry - thing in my time of need.

To Coda
E♭
F
You are ev - 'ry - thing,
You are ev - 'ry - thing I
E♭
E♭add2(♯4)
Gm7
need.
When ev - er - y mo - ment is
mf
B♭
E♭
more than I can take,
and all of my strength is
Gm7
slip - ping a - way,
when ev - er - y breath gets

B♭
E♭
3fr
Fsus
D.S. al Coda
hard - er to breathe, You car - ry me. Je - sus, car - ry me.
CODA
F
Gm7
B♭
You are ev - 'ry - thing I need.
E♭
3fr
Gm7
You, You are ev - 'ry - thing I need.
B♭
E♭
3fr
I love ev - 'ry - thing a - bout You.

F
Gm7
E♭
B♭
3fr
You are strength in my weak - ness, You are the
mp
Fsus
F
B♭
F
Gm7
ref - uge I seek. You are ev - 'ry - thing in my time of need.
f
E♭
F
You are ev - 'ry - thing, You are ev - 'ry - thing.
B♭
F
Gm7
E♭
B♭
You are strength in my weak - ness, and You are the

F Gm7 B♭ F Gm7
ref - uge I ___ seek. You are ev - 'ry - thing in my time of need. ___
E♭ 3fr F
___ You are ev - 'ry - thing, ___ You are ev - 'ry - thing I
E♭ 3fr F E♭(add2) 6fr
need. Ev - 'ry - thing, ___ You are ev - 'ry - thing I need.
mf
E♭maj7 3fr

GET BACK UP

Words and Music by TOBY McKEEHAN,
JAMIE MOORE, AARON RICE
and CARY BARLOWE

A♭
4fr
E♭
3fr
B♭
Fm
Seems like you're fight-ing for your life, but why, oh why?
It feels like you've been run-ning all your life, but why, oh why? So you
A♭
4fr
E♭
3fr
B♭
Cm
3fr
Wide a-wake in the mid-dle of your night-mare, you saw it com-ing, but it hit you out of no-where.
pull a-way from the love that would-'ve been there, and start be-liev-ing that your sit-u-a-tion's un-fair.
Fm7
A♭
4fr
And there's al-ways scars when you fall that far. We
But there's al-ways scars when you fall that far.
E♭
3fr
Cm7
3fr
A♭
4fr
lose our way, we get back up a-gain. It's nev-er too late to get back up a-gain.

E♭
3fr
Fm
A♭
4fr
And one day you gon' shine _ a-gain. You may be knocked down, but not _ out for-ev - er. We
E♭
3fr
Cm
3fr
A♭
4fr
lose our way, we get back up _ a-gain, so get up, get up, you gon' shine _ a-gain. It's
E♭
3fr
Fm
A♭
4fr
nev-er too late to get back up _ a-gain. You may be knocked down, but not _ out for-ev - er,
1
E♭
3fr
may be knocked down, but not _ out for-ev - er.

2
Fm
A♭
4fr
Cm
3fr
B♭
may be knocked down, but not out for - ev - er.
This is love call - ing, love call - ing
out to the bro - ken, this is love call - ing.
This is love call - ing, love call - ing
out to the bro - ken, this is love call - ing.

Fm
Cm
3fr
B♭
This is love call - ing, love call - ing.
I am so bro - ken. This is love call - ing, love call - ing.
E♭
B♭/D
We lose our way, we
A♭
4fr
get back up a - gain, (get back up a - gain.) It's nev - er too late. You

Fm
A♭
4fr
E♭
3fr
may be knocked down, but not out for - ev - er. We lose our way, we get back up a - gain.
Cm
3fr
A♭
4fr
E♭
3fr
So get up, get up, you gon' shine a - gain. It's nev - er too late to get back up a - gain. You
Fm
A♭
4fr
E♭
3fr
This is love call - ing, love call - ing
may be knocked down, but not out for - ev - er. We lose our way, we
Cm
3fr
A♭
4fr
E♭
3fr
out to the bro - ken, this is love call - ing.
get back up a - gain, get back up a - gain. It's nev - er too late. You

Fm
Ab
4fr
Eb
3fr
This is love call - ing, love call - ing
may be knocked down, but not out for - ev - er. We lose our way, we
Cm
3fr
Ab
4fr
Eb
3fr
out to the bro - ken, this is love call - ing.
get back up a - gain, get back up a - gain. It's nev - er too late. You
Fm
Ab
4fr
Eb5
6fr
may be knocked down, but not out for - ev - er.
This is love call - ing, love call - ing
C5
3fr
Ab5
4fr
Eb5
6fr
Ab5
4fr
Eb5
6fr
out to the bro - ken, this is love call - ing.

COME HOME

Words and Music by BEN GLOVER,
SAM HANCOCK, CODY CLARK, DUSTIN DELONG,
DUSTY JAKUBIK and AARON MATTHEW

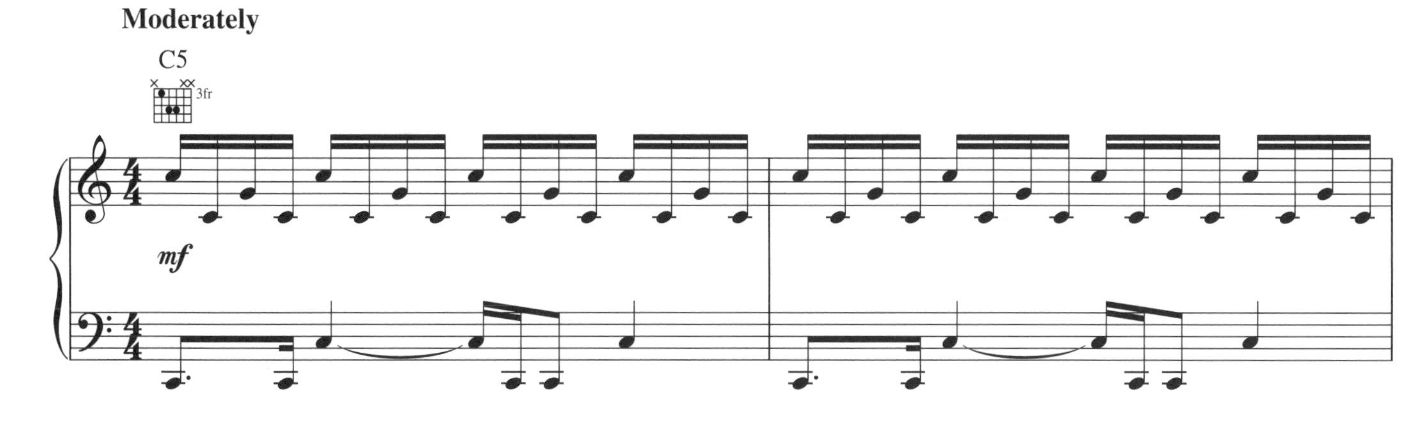

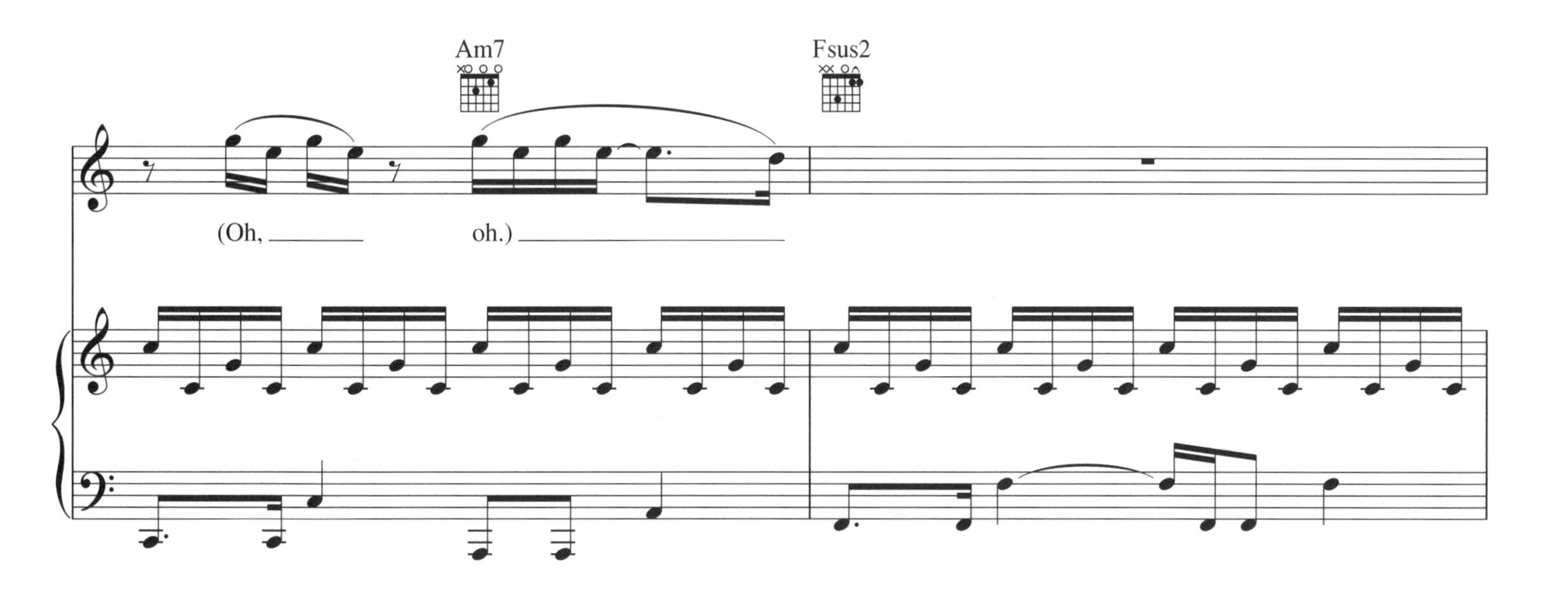

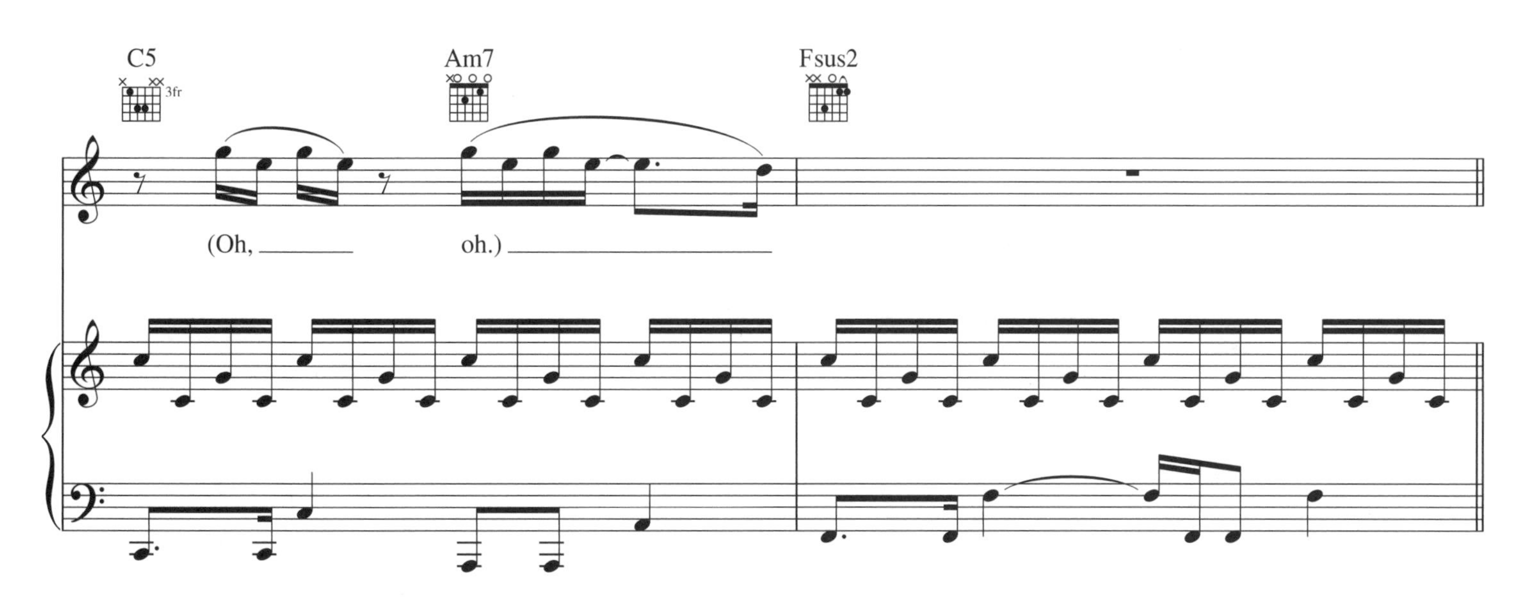

C
Am7
Fsus2
You're best friends with the word re - gret,
and you're a - fraid that your life's been wast - ed.
You can try to fix your bro - ken em - pire
and put bricks on a cracked foun - da - tion,
C
Am7
Fsus2
So why hope if it's on - ly gon - na let you down?
but you'll be build - ing cas - tles on the sand.
C
Am7
Fsus2
You don't think peo - ple real - ly change.
You're a mess and you'll al - ways be the same,
There's pow'r in the blood of Je - sus,
and your Fa - ther's scream - ing, "Just come home!"
C
Am7
Fsus2
and you doubt if you'll ev - er get it turned a - round.
So, you've been run -
And He's reach - ing out His hands.
I know you've been run -

C
G
- ning, ___
- ning, ___
search - ing for some - thing, ___ but you're look -
Am7
F
- ing in ___ a place _ you don't _ be - long. ___ But it's nev - er too _
C
Em7
___ late; ___ you can't out - run grace. _ No, mer -
Am7
1
F
- cy does - n't care ___ what _ you've done, ___ so come _ home, _

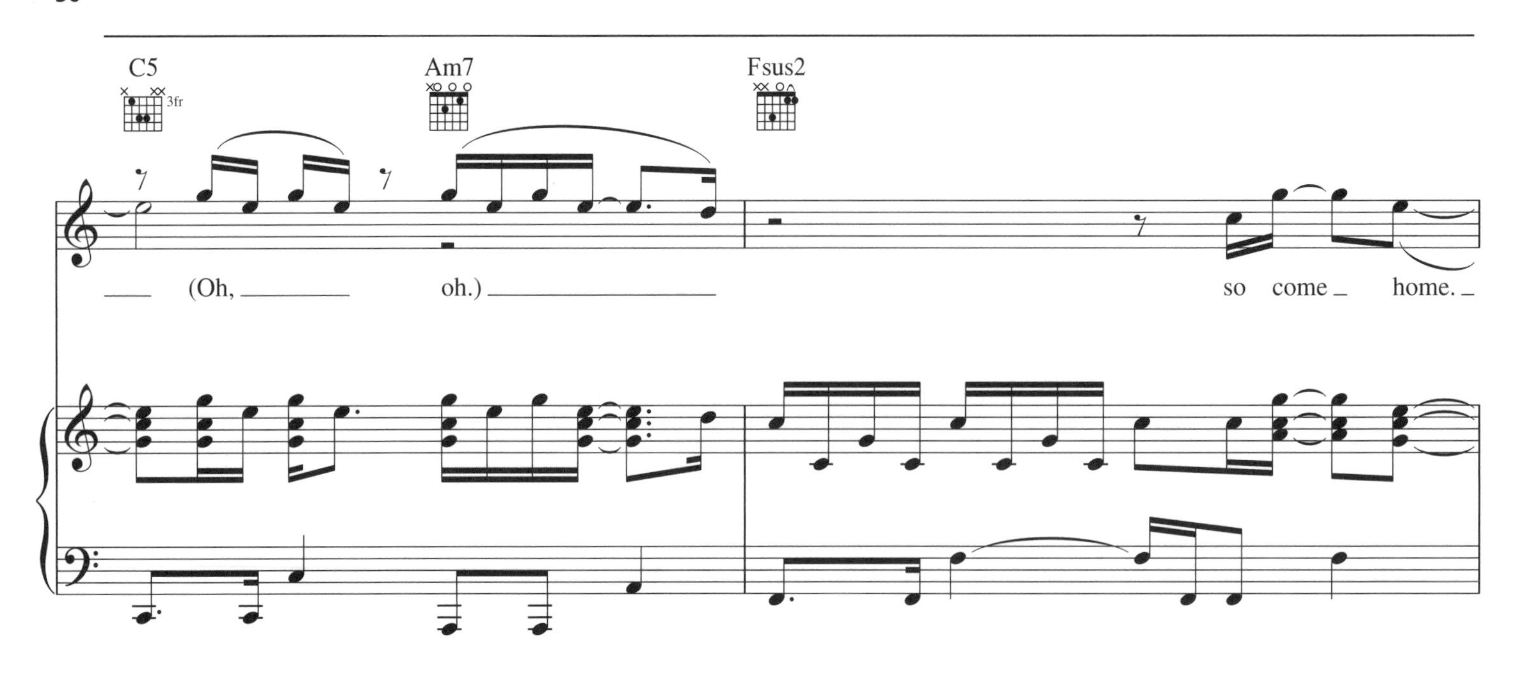
C5
3fr
Am7
Fsus2
(Oh, oh.)
so come home.

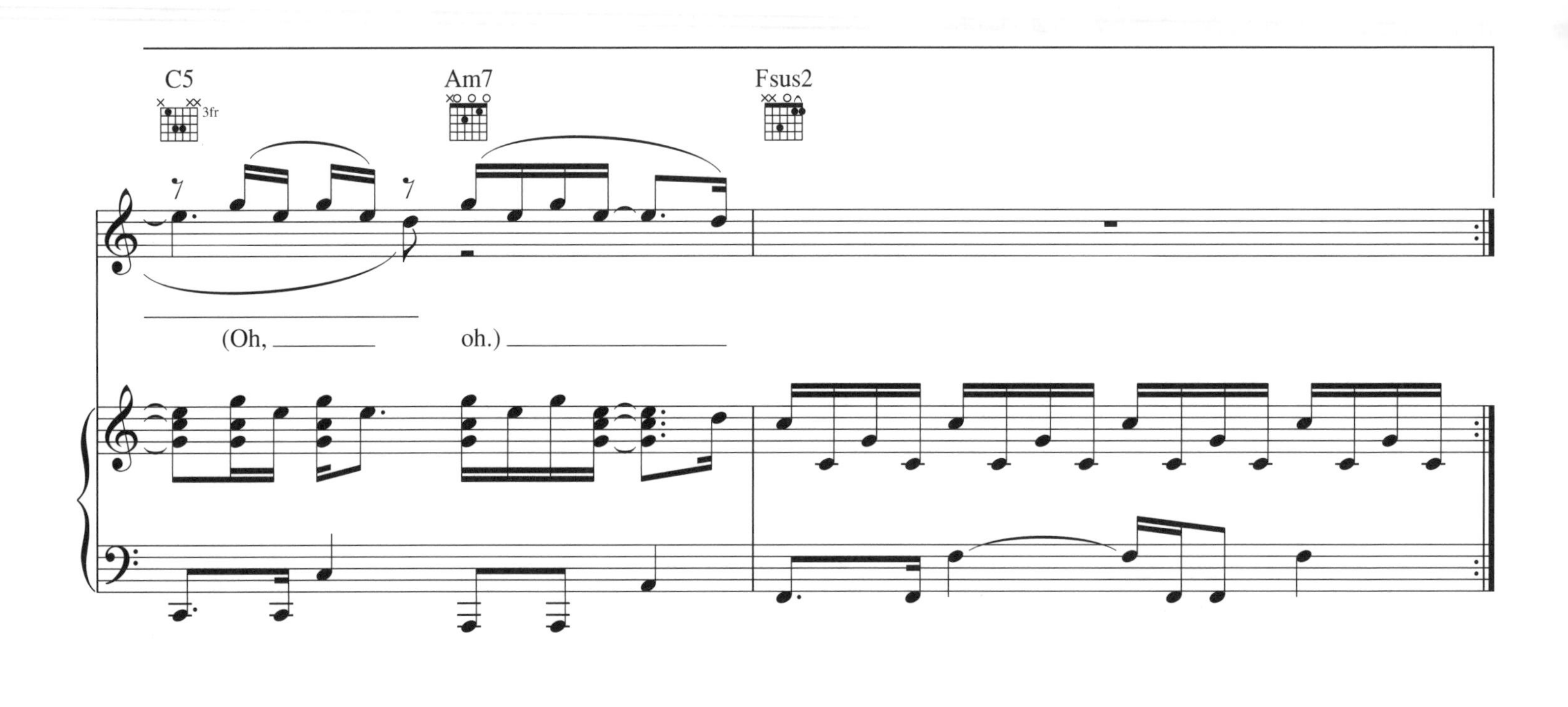
C5
3fr
Am7
Fsus2
(Oh, oh.)

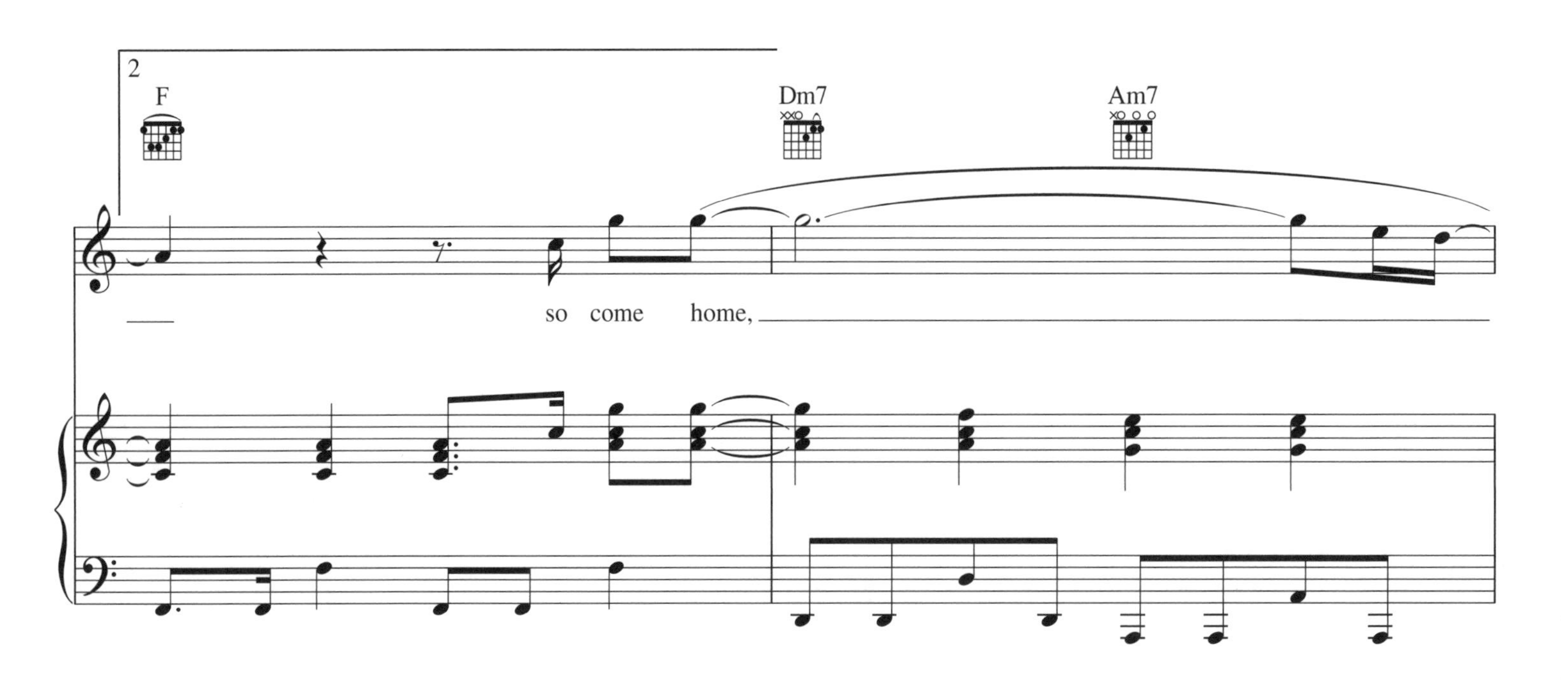
2
F
Dm7
Am7
so come home,

G
Dm7
Am7
so come home.
G
Dm7
F
From the shad - ows, from the wrong roads,
G
Dm7
Am7
from the dark - ness, from the un - known. To re - demp - tion, some - thing beau - ti - ful,
G
to a new love, to a new home. I know you've been run -

C
G
- ning, search-ing for some - thing, but you're look -
Am7
F
- ing in a place you don't be - long.
And it's nev - er too
C
Em7
late; you can't out - run grace.
No, mer -
Am7
F
- cy does - n't care what you've done,
so come home,

C
Am7
Fsus2
(Oh,
oh.)
so come
home.
C
Am7
Fsus2
(Oh,
oh.)
Yeah!
C5
3fr
Am7
Fsus2
(Oh,
oh.)
C5
3fr
Am7
Fsus2
Repeat and Fade
Optional Ending
C
(Oh,
oh.)

GOD GAVE ME YOU

Words and Music by
DAVE BARNES

C#m
B7sus
F#m7(add4)
4fr
2fr
and watch as the storm blows through. And I need you.
I'll be the flat - tered fool. But I need you.
Asus2
Bsus
Asus2
E
God gave me you for the ups and downs.
C#m
Bsus
Asus2
E
God gave me you for the days of doubt.
C#m
Bsus
Asus2
E
For when I think I've lost my way, there are no words

C♯m
Bsus
F♯m7(add4)
To Coda
here left to say. It's true:
1
Asus2
Bsus
Asus2
E5
God gave me you.
C♯m
B(add4)
Asus2
E5
C♯m
B(add4)
2
Asus2
Bsus
God gave me you.

C♯m
4fr
Asus2
On my own, I'm on - ly half of what I could be. I
E
B
can't do with - out you.
C♯m
4fr
Asus2
We are stitched to - geth - er; and what love has teth - ered, I
E
B
pray we nev - er un - do. God

N.C.
gave me you for the ups and downs.
God
D.S. al Coda
gave me you for the days of doubt.
God
CODA
Asus2
Bsus
Asus2
E5
God gave me you,
C♯m
4fr
B(add4)
Asus2
E5
gave me you,

C♯m
B(add4)
Asus2
E5
gave _ me you.
C♯m
B(add4)
Asus2
E5
C♯m
B(add4)
Asus2
Repeat and Fade
Optional Ending
L.H.

HEALING BEGINS

Words and Music by JASON INGRAM,
MIKE DONEHEY and JEFF OWEN

Gsus2
D/F♯
G
A
on the out - side. So let them fall down. There's
D/F♯
G
A
D/F♯
G
free - dom wait - ing in the sound when you let your walls fall to the ground.
A
D/F♯
G
A7
We're here now.
Bm
G
D
A
Bm
G
This is where the heal - ing be - gins, oh. This is where the heal - ing starts.
mf – f

D
A
Bm
G
When you come to where you're bro - ken with - in, the light meets the
dark, the light meets the dark.
To Coda
Dsus2
A - fraid to let your se - crets out;
Asus
Bm7
ev - 'ry - thing that you hide could come crash -
mp
mf

Gsus2
D
- ing through the door now, but too scared to face all your fear.
Asus
Bm7
G
So you hide, but you find that the shame won't dis - ap - pear.
D/F♯
G
A
D/F♯
G
So let them fall down. There's free - dom wait - ing in the sound
A
D/F♯
G
A
when you let your walls fall to the ground. We're here now.

D/F♯
G
A
D/F♯
G
We're here now, oh.
A
D.S. al Coda
cresc.
CODA
D
A
Em7
Sparks will fly
D/F♯
G
A
as grace col - lides with the dark in - side of us.
Em7
D/F♯
G
So please don't fight this com - ing light. Let this blood

A
Em7
D/F♯
come cov - er us.
His blood can cov - er us.
G6
A
D/F♯
G
mp
A
D/F♯
G
Esus
Bm
G
D
A
Bm
G
This is where the heal - ing be - gins,
oh.
This is where the heal - ing starts.
f

D
A
Bm
G
When you come to where you're bro - ken with - in,
the light meets the dark,
the light meets the
dark.
D5
5fr
mf

HOLD US TOGETHER

Words and Music by STEVE WILSON
and MATT MAHER

Am F C G/B Am F
in five eas - y steps.
C E7 Am F C F
Ain't the law of the land or the gov - ern - ment,
C G C/G G7
but it's all you need.
on your knees.
And love
C G Am F C F
will hold us to - geth - er, make us a shel - ter to weath-

Am F C G/B Am F
- er the storm. And I'll be my broth - er's keep - er so the
To Coda
C F G C G
whole world will know that we're not a - lone. It's wait-ing for you,
Am F C G Am F
knock-ing at your door
C E7 Am F C
D.S. al Coda
in the mo - ment of truth when your heart hits the floor and you're

CODA
G
C
G
a - lone. This is the first day of the
Am
F
C
G
Am
F
rest of your life. This is the first day of the rest of your life. 'Cause
C
E7
Am
F
e - ven in the dark, you can still see the light. It's gon - na be al -
C
F
1
C
G
- right, it's gon - na be al - right. This is the

2
C G C G Am F
- right. And love will hold us to-geth - er, make
C F Am F
us a shel - ter to weath - er the storm. And I'll
C G/B Am F
be my broth - er's keep - er so the
C Am F C/E Dm7 C
whole world will know that we're not a - lone.
rit.

HUMAN

Words and Music by JASON INGRAM,
DANIEL MUCKALA and JORDIN SPARKS

A♭sus2
3fr
B♭sus
3
3
and we are called to be hu - man. We
A♭
4fr
E♭
3fr
B♭
Cm
3fr
got - ta do bet - ter than this, 'cause we've on - ly got one chance to make a dif - fer - ence.
f
A♭
E♭
B♭
Cm
Got - ta do bet - ter than this, 'cause we've on - ly got one life that we've been giv - en.
A♭
E♭
B♭
Cm
A lit - tle love, a lit - tle kind - ness, a lit - tle light in this time of dark - ness.

A♭
4fr
E♭
3fr
B♭
It - 'll be what makes us dif - fer - ent, it - 'll be what makes us hu - man.
I'm hu - man, you're hu - man, we are, we are hu - man.
To Coda
I'm hu - man, you're hu - man, we are, we are hu - man.
Gm/D
Cm
3
We are marked with His im - age,
mf

E♭
Gm/D
Cm
3fr
but we are scarred with in - dif - f'rence.
E♭
Gm/D
Cm
May - be now we should lis - ten,
E♭
A♭
B♭sus
4fr
D.S. al Coda
hear the cry of God's chil - dren. We
CODA
B♭
A♭
E♭
we are, we are hu - man.
I've got - ta do bet - ter than this, 'cause I've on - ly got
mp

B♭
Cm7
A♭
E♭
B♭
one chance to make a dif-fer-ence. Got-ta do bet-ter than this,'cause I'm on-ly just one.
B♭
F
C
Dm7
I'm hu - man, you're hu - man, we are, we are hu - man.
B♭
F
C
Dm7
I'm hu - man, you're hu - man, we are, we are hu - man.
B♭
F
C
Dm
A lit - tle love, a lit - tle kind - ness, a lit - tle light in this time of dark - ness.

B♭
F
C
It - 'll be what makes us dif - fer - ent. We are, we are hu - man.
Oh, oh, oh, we are hu - man. Oh, oh,
oh, we are hu - man. It - 'll be what makes the dif - fer - ence,
it - 'll be what makes us hu - man.
mf
3

I WILL FOLLOW

Words and Music by CHRIS TOMLIN,
REUBEN MORGAN and JASON INGRAM

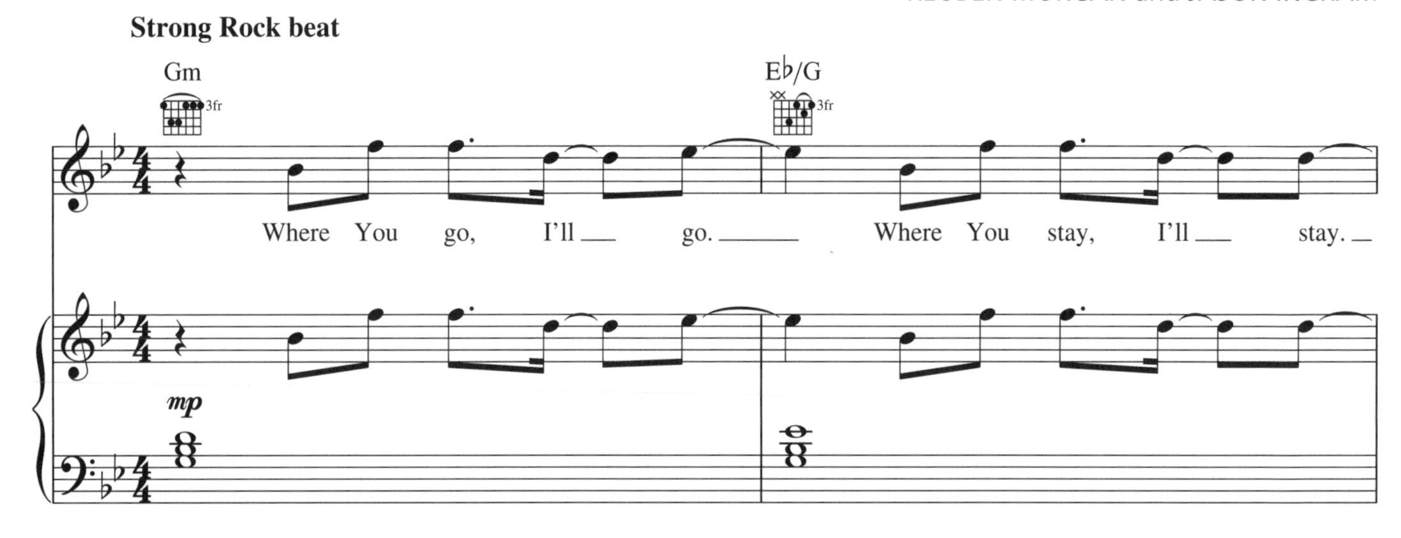

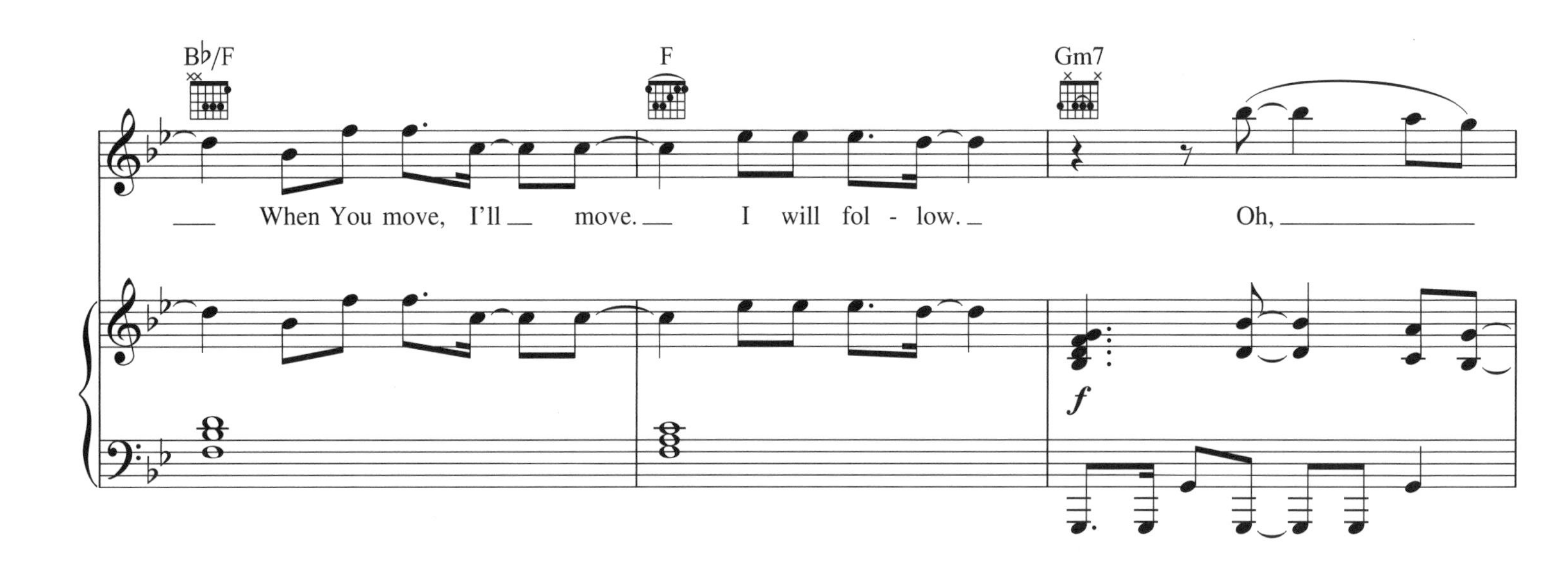

E♭
3fr
Gm7
All Your ways are good, all Your ways are sure.
Light un - to the world, Light un - to my life,
mf
F
B♭
F/A
I will trust in You a - lone.
I will live for You a - lone.
E♭
3fr
Gm7
High - er than my sight, high a - bove my life,
You're the One I seek, know - ing I will find
F
B♭
F/A
I will trust in You a - lone.
all I need in You a - lone,

E♭
3fr
Fsus
F
in You a - lone.
Gm7
E♭
3fr
Where You go, I'll go. Where You stay, I'll stay.
f
B♭
F
When You move, I'll move. I will fol - low You.
Gm7
E♭
3fr
Who You love, I'll love. How You serve, I'll serve.

B♭
F
If this life I lose, I will fol - low You,
Gm7
E♭
3fr
yeah.
I will fol - low You,
B♭
1
F
2
F
yeah.
E♭maj9
B♭
F
E♭maj9
In You, there's life ev - er - last - ing. In You, there's
mf

B♭
F
E♭maj9
B♭
F
free - dom for my soul. In You, there's joy, un - end - ing
E♭maj9
Gm7
joy, and I will fol - low. Where You go, I'll go.
mp
E♭
3fr
B♭
F
Where You stay, I'll stay. When You move, I'll move. I will fol - low.
Gm7
E♭
3fr
B♭
Who You love, I'll love. How You serve, I'll serve. If this life I lose,

F
Gm7
I will fol - low.
Where You go, I'll go.
E♭
3fr
B♭
Where You stay, I'll stay.
When You move, I'll move.
F
Gm7
I will fol - low You.
Who You love, I'll love.
E♭
3fr
B♭
How You serve, I'll serve.
If this life I lose,
f

F
Gm7
I will fol - low You, yeah.
Eb
3fr
Bb
I will fol - low You, yeah.
F
Gm7
I will fol - low You, yeah.
Eb
3fr
Bb
F
I will fol - low You, yeah.

LIFT UP YOUR FACE

Words by MAC POWELL
Music by MAC POWELL, TAI ANDERSON, DAVID CARR,
MARK LEE, BEAR RINEHART and BO RINEHART

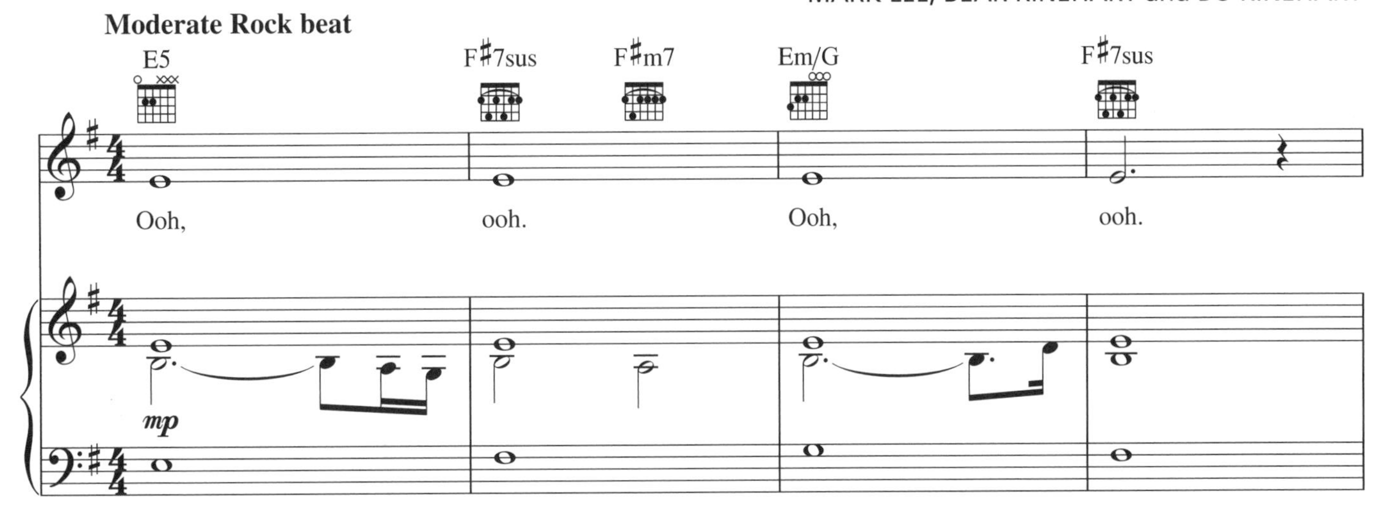

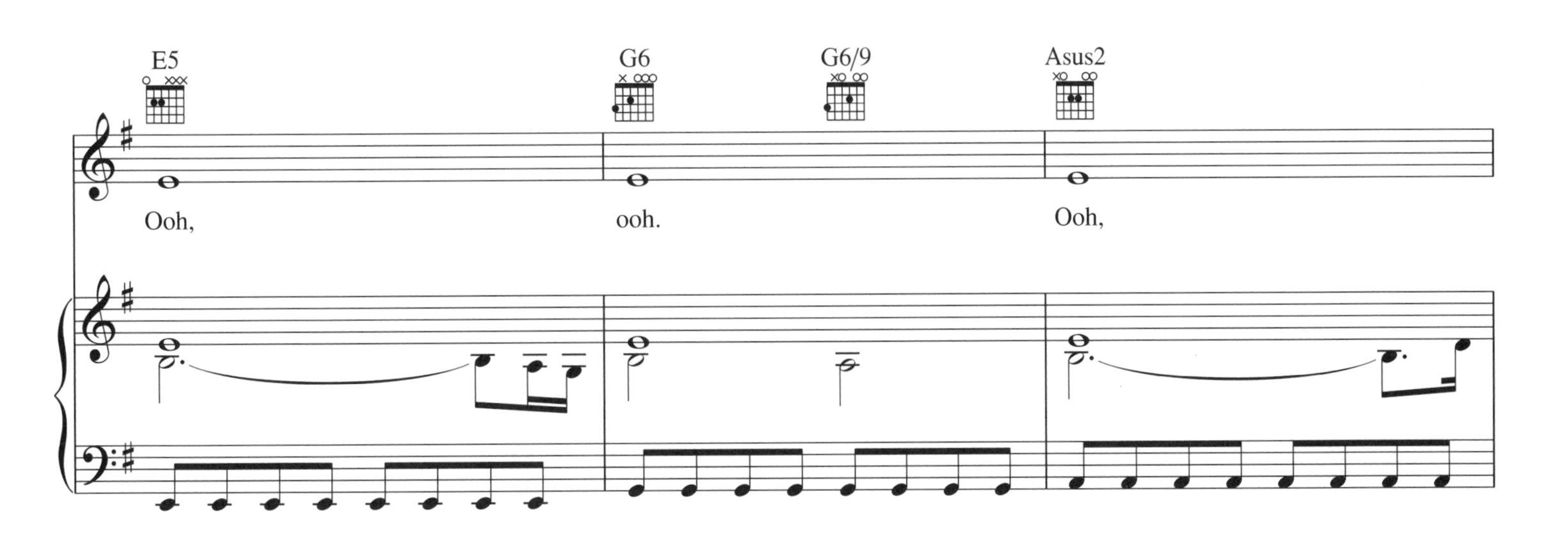

Asus2
Bsus
E5
va - tion is call - ing, sal - va - tion is call - ing.
f
G6
A5
5fr
Bsus
B
E
Am7
C
You have fall - en so far now, you don't e - ven know how you are
mf
G
D/F#
E
Am7
go - ing to sur - vive. But just o - ver the ho - ri - zon, a new light is shin -

C G D/F♯ C
- ing, break-ing through the dark - est night. Love is com-ing and it's
Am Bsus Em G
call-ing out your name. Lift up your face, lift up your face. Sal -
Am Bsus B Em
va-tion is call - ing, sal - va-tion is call-ing. Lift up your face,
G Am Bsus B
lift up your face. Sal - va-tion is call - ing, sal - va-tion is call-ing your name.

E5 E Am7
You feel like your life is fad - ing, you're tired of wait -
mf
C G D/F♯ E
- ing for your mo - ment to ar - rive. But to - mor-row will bring
Am7 C G D/F♯
a song that you can sing, and your hope is gon - na rise.
C Bsus Em
Love is com-ing and it's call-ing out your name. Lift up your face,
f

G6
Am
Bsus
B
lift up your face.
Sal - va - tion is call - ing,
sal - va - tion is call - ing.
Em
G6
Am
Lift up your face,
lift up your face.
Sal - va - tion is call - ing,
sal -
Bsus
Em
Am
va - tion is call - ing your name.
C
Bsus
Bm
Em

Am
C
Bsus
E5
mf
Ooh,
1
2
ooh.
Em
G6
Am
f
Lift up your face,
lift up your face.
Sal - va - tion is call - ing, sal -
(Vocal ad lib. on repeat)

Bsus
Em
G6
va - tion is call - ing. Lift up your face, lift up your face. Sal -
Am
1
Bsus
2
Bsus
va - tion is call - ing, sal - va - tion is call - ing your name. va - tion is call - ing your name.
E
Am
Just o - ver the ho - ri - zon, a new light is shin -
mf
C
G
D/F♯
E
- ing. Sal - va - tion is on its way.
rit.

IF WE'VE EVER NEEDED YOU

Words and Music by MARK HALL
and BERNIE HERMS

D
F♯m
With ship - wrecked faith, the i - dols rise.
All our hearts, all our strength,
mf
D
F♯m
We do what is right in our own eyes.
with all our minds, we're at Your feet.
D
A
Our chil - dren now will pay the price.
May Your king - dom come in our hearts and lives.
Em/G
A
We need Your light, Lord, shine Your light.
Let Your church a - rise, let Your church a - rise.

D
F♯m7
If we've ev - er need - ed You, Lord, it's
Gsus2
A
now, Lord, it's now.
D
F♯m7
We are des - p'rate for Your hand. We're reach - ing out.
1
Gsus2
A
We're reach - ing out.

2
Gsus2
A
We're reach - ing out.
D/F♯
G
A
Bm7
D
We're reach - ing out.
A
Gsus2
Em7
D
F♯m7
mp
If we've ev - er need - ed You, Lord, it's

Gsus2
A
now, Lord, it's now.
D
F♯m7
We are des - p'rate for Your hand. We're reach - ing out.
mf
G
A
We're reach - ing out.
D
F♯m7
If we've ev - er need - ed You, Lord, it's

Gsus2
A
D
now, Lord, it's now.
We are des-p'rate for Your
F♯m7
Gsus2
hand. We're reach - ing out.
We're reach - ing out.
A
Gsus2
A
We need You now.
Re - vive us
mp
G
A
Gsus2
now.
We need You now.

JESUS SAVES

Words and Music by TIM HUGHES
and NICK HERBERT

With energy

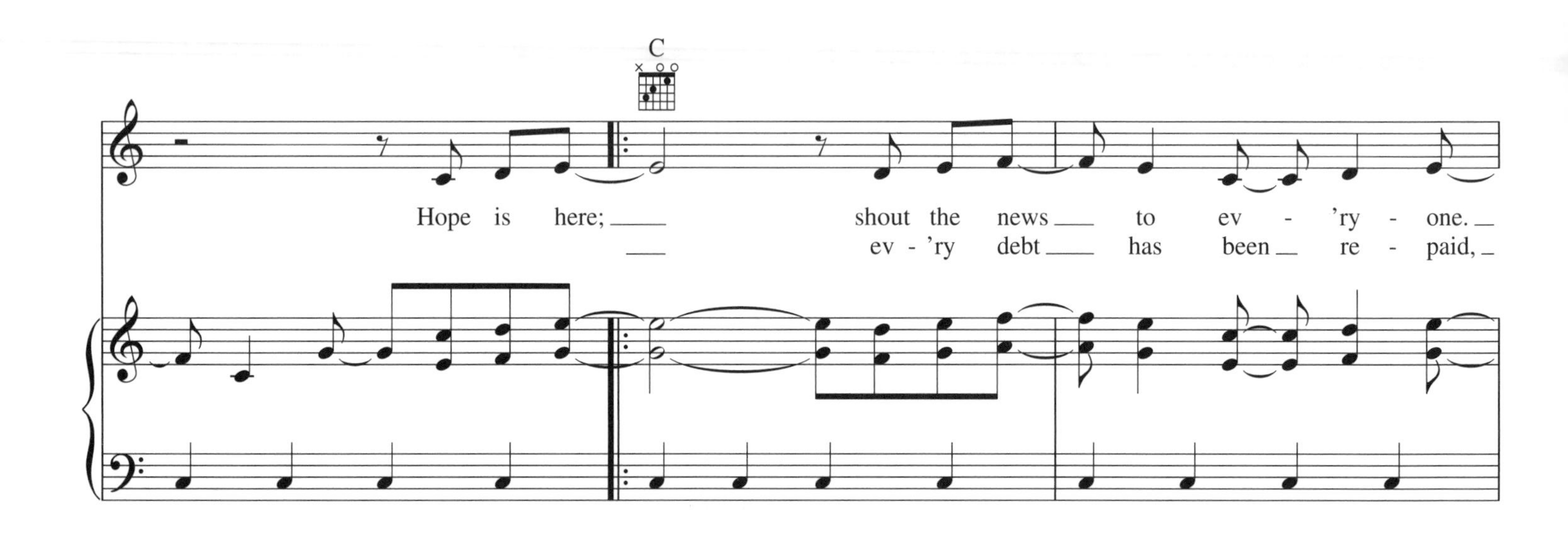

* Recorded a half step lower.

F
C
Je - sus saves. Mer - cy tri - umphs at the cross,
Je - sus saves. Sing a - bove the storms of life,
love has come to res - cue us.
sing it through the dark - est night.
Am7
F
C
Je - sus saves. Hope is here;
Je - sus saves. Free at last;
F
G
F
what a joy - ful noise we'll make as we join

Am7
G
Am7
with heav - en's song
to let all the world know that
F
C
G
Je - sus saves!
Raise a shout
to let
Am7
F
1
C
all the world know that Je - sus saves!
Free at last;
2, 3
C
G
Am7
Sing it out
Shout it out
to let all the world know that

F
C/E
G
Je - sus saves! Raise a shout to let
Am7
F
To Coda
C
all the world know that Je - sus saves! You save,
G
C/E
You heal, re - store, re - veal Your Fa -
F
G
- ther's heart to us. You rose to raise us from

C/E
F
C/E
Dm7
the grave; Your Spir - it lives in us.
D.S. al Coda
(take 2nd ending)
Sing it out
CODA
C
Sing it out
G
Am7
F
to let all the world know that Je - sus saves!
C
G
Am7
Raise a shout to let all the world know that

F
C
G
Je - sus saves! Oh, sing it out and shout 'til the whole
Am7
F
C
world knows His name. Je - sus! Sing it out
G
Am7
F
and shout, for we will know Your name.
Dm7
C/E
F6/9
Je - sus.

LEAD ME

Words and Music by JASON INGRAM,
MATT HAMMITT and CHRIS ROHMAN

* *Recorded a half step higher.*

Am7
I see my beau - ti - ful wife always smil - ing.
I tell my - self they'll be fine; they're in - de - pend - ent.
G
But on the in - side, oh, I can hear
But on the in - side, oh, I can hear
her say - ing:
them say - ing:
C
Lead me with
G
strong hands, stand up when

F
I can't. Don't leave me hun - gry for love, chas - ing
Am
G
C
dreams, but what a - bout us? Show me you're
G
will - ing to fight, that I'm still the love of your life. I
F
Am
know we call this our home, but I still feel

G
1
C
a - lone.
2
C
Dm7
So Fa - ther, give me the strength
F
C
G
to be ev - 'ry - thing I'm called to be. Oh, Fa -
Dm7
F
C
- ther, show me the way to lead them.

G
Won't You lead me to
C
G
lead them with strong hands, to stand up when
mp
F
they can't. Don't wan - na leave them hun - gry for love, chas - ing
Am
G
C
things that I could give up. I'll show them I'm
cresc.
mf

G
will - ing to fight and give them the best of my life, so
F
Am
we can call this our home. Lead me, 'cause I
G
C
can't do this a - lone. Fa - ther, lead
Am
G
C
me, 'cause I can't do this a - lone.

LET THE WATERS RISE

Words and Music by BEN GLOVER,
MIKE GRAYSON and SAM TINNESZ

G
Some - times it's so hard to pray when You feel so far a - way,
God, You know where I've been, and You were there with me then.
Em
but I am will - ing to go where you want me to.
You were faith - ful be - fore, You'll be faith - ful a - gain.
C
God, I trust You.
I'm hold - ing Your hand.
Em
There's a rag - ing sea
C
right in front of me,

G
D
wants to pull me in, bring me to my knees.
Em
C
So let the wa - ters rise if You want them to.
G
D
Em
I will fol - low You, I will fol - low You.
C
G
D
(D.C.)
I will fol - low You.

Em
Cmaj7
God, Your love is e - nough, You will pull me through,
G
D/F♯
I'm hold - ing on to You.
Em
Cmaj7
God, Your love is e - nough, I will fol - low You,
G
D/F♯
I will fol - low You.

Em
C
(Oh, oh, oh, oh, oh, oh,
G
D/F♯
oh, oh, oh.)
Em
C
There's a rag - ing sea right in front of me,
G
D
wants to pull me in, bring me to my knees.

Em
C
G
So let the wa-ters rise if You want them to. I will fol-low You,
D
Em
C
I will fol-low You. I will fol-low You.
G
D
Em
(Oh, oh, oh,
C
G
D
oh, oh, oh, oh, oh, oh.)

LIGHT UP THE SKY

Words and Music by JASON INGRAM,
DANIEL MUCKALA, MATT FUQUA
and JOSH HAVENS

Bm
G
D
A
When the night is clos - ing in,
is fall - ing on my skin,
when I've al - most reached the end,
like a flood You're rush - ing in,
Bm
G
D
O God, will You come close?
Your love is rush - ing in.
Bm
G
D
A/D
Light, light, light up the sky,
You light up the sky to show me You are with me.
mf
Bm
G
D
A/D
I, I, I can't de - ny,
no, I can't de - ny that You are right here with me. You've

Bm G D A

o - pened my eyes so I can see You all a - round me.

Bm G D

Light, light, light up the sky, You light up the sky to show me that You are with

1

Bm G D

me.

2

Bm7 G D

me. So I

Em
Bm
A
run straight in - to Your arms.
You're the bright and morn - ing sun.
Em
G
To show Your love, there's noth - ing You won't do.
G
D
Light, light, light up the sky, You light up the sky
f
A
Bm
G
D
to show me You are with me. I, I, I can't de - ny, no, I can't de - ny

A
Bm
G
D
that You are right here with me. You've o - pened my eyes so
3
3

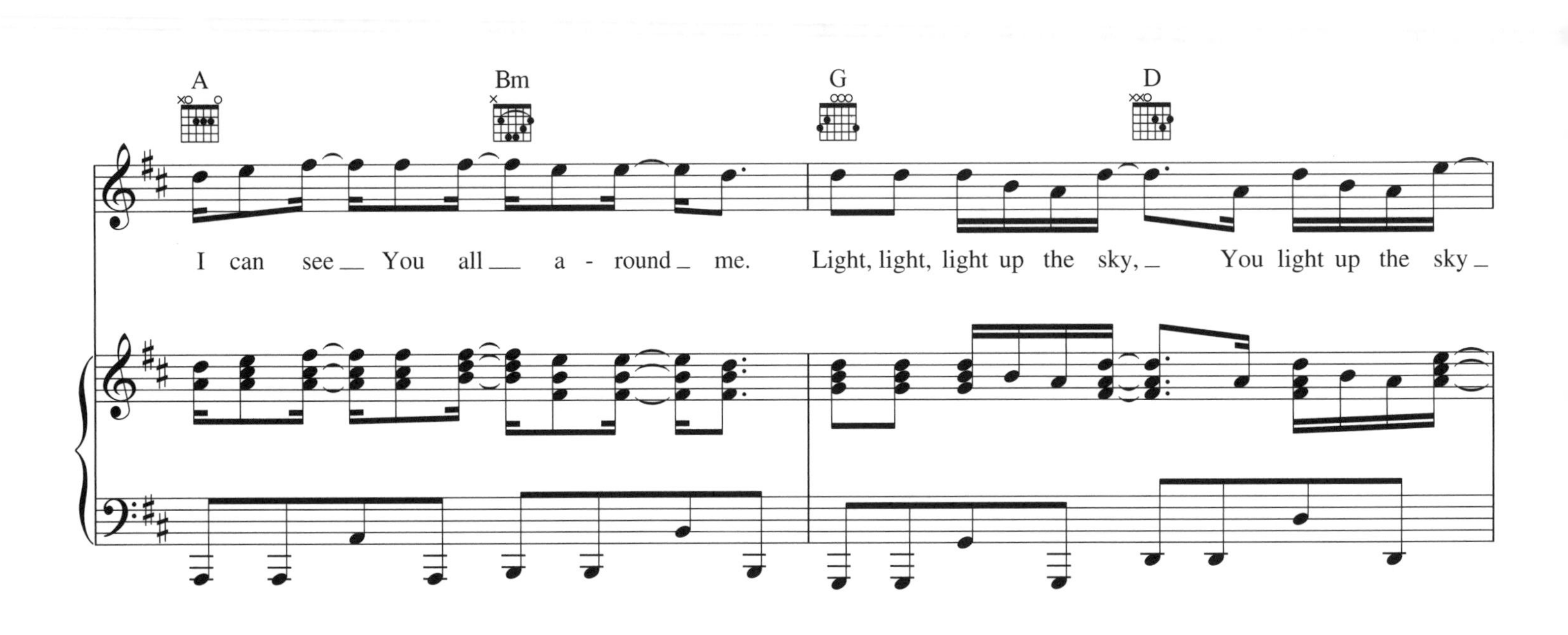
A
Bm
G
D
I can see You all a - round me. Light, light, light up the sky, You light up the sky

A
G
D
to show me that You are with me,
(Oh, oh, oh, oh,

A
Bm
G
D
that You are with me,
oh, oh.)
(Oh, oh, oh, oh,

A
Bm
G
D
that You are with me.
oh, oh.)
(Oh, oh, oh, oh,

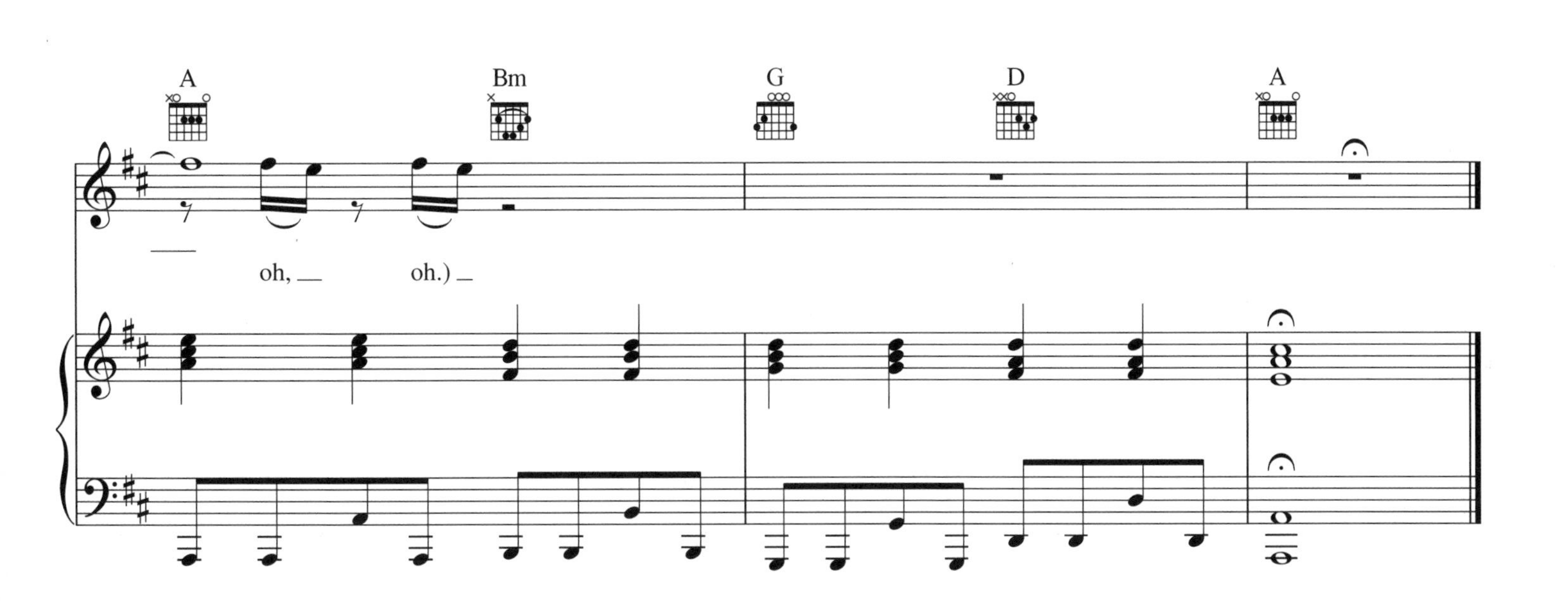
A
Bm
G
D
A
oh, oh.)

NO MATTER WHAT

Words and Music by CHUCK BUTLER,
KERRIE ROBERTS and TONY WOOD

F
C
en me by sur - prise, but noth -
it with - out Your help; I won't
Gm
3fr
B♭
ing sur - pris - es You. Be - fore a heart - ache
e - ven try it. I know You have Your rea - sons
F
C
can ev - er touch my life, it has
for ev - 'ry - thing, so I
Gm
3fr
B♭
to go through Your hands. And e - ven though I
will keep be - liev - ing, what - ev - er I might be feel - ing,

F C

keep ask - ing why, I keep ask - ing why.
God, You are my hope, and You'll be my strength.

Gm 3fr Bb

No mat - ter what, I'm gon - na love

F C Gm 3fr

You. No mat - ter what, I'm gon - na need You. I know that You

Bb F C To Coda

can find a way to keep me from the pain. But if not, if not, I'll trust

Gm7
Dm
You, no mat - ter what,
No mat - ter, no mat - ter what,
C
Gm
Dm
no mat - ter what.
no mat - ter, no mat - ter what, no mat - ter, no mat - ter what.
1
2
C
C
Gm
3fr
F
No mat - ter, no mat - ter what. An - y - thing I don't have,
C/E
F
C/E
B♭
You can give it to me, but it's o - kay if You don't.

Gm
F
C/E
F
C/E
3fr
I'm not here for those things; the touch of Your love is e - nough on it's own.
B♭
And no mat - ter what, I still love
F
C
Gm
3fr
D.S. al Coda
You, and I'm gon - na need You. No mat - ter what,
CODA
Gm7
B♭
You. I know that You can find a way to keep me

F
C
from the pain. But if not, but if not, I'll trust
Gm7
Dm
C
You, no mat-ter what.
No mat-ter, no mat-ter what, no mat-ter, no mat-ter what.
Gm
3fr
Dm
C
Gm
3fr
Dm
No mat-ter, no mat-ter what, no mat-ter, no mat-ter what. No mat-ter, no mat-ter what,
C
Gm
3fr
Dm
C
no mat-ter, no mat-ter what. No mat-ter, no mat-ter what.

OUR GOD

Words and Music by JONAS MYRIN,
CHRIS TOMLIN, MATT REDMAN
and JESSE REEVES

* Recorded a half step lower.

Dm7
Gsus
3fr
G
like You, none like You.
Am
F
C
Am
F
In - to the dark - ness You shine, out of the ash - es we rise.
mf
C
Dm7
There's no one like You, none like
Gsus
3fr
G
𝄋
Am
You. Our God is great - er,

F
C
G/B
our God is strong - er. God, You are high - er than an - y oth - er.
Am
F
C
To Coda
Our God is Heal - er, awe-some in pow - er, our God, our God.
1
G
Am
F
C
Gsus
3fr
2
G
D.S. al Coda

CODA
G
Am
F
gradual cresc.
C
G
Am
F
C
G
Am
F
C
And if our God is for us, then who could ev - er stop us? And if our God is with us,
f

G
Am
F
then what could stand a - gainst? And if our God is for us, then who could ev - er stop us?
C
Gsus
3fr
Am7
And if our God is with us, then what could stand a - gainst?
ff
Fsus2
C/E
Gsus
3fr
What could stand a - gainst?
Am7
Fsus2
C/E

Gsus
3fr
Am7
Fsus2
Our God is great - er, our God is strong - er.
f
C
G/B
Am7
God, You are high - er than an - y oth - er. Our God is Heal - er,
Fsus2
C
1
Gsus
3fr
awe-some in pow - er, our God, our God.
3
3
3
3
2
Gsus
3fr
Am7
Fsus2
And if our God is for us, then who could ev - er stop us?

C
Gsus
3fr
And if our God is with us,
then what could stand a - gainst? _
Am7
Fsus2
C
___ And if our God is for us,
then who could ev - er stop us?
And if our God is with us,
Gsus
3fr
Am7
Fsus2
then what could stand a - gainst? _
ff
C/E
Gsus
3fr
Am7
Then what could stand a - gainst? ___

Fsus2
C/E
Gsus
3fr
Am
F
C
Our God is great - er, our God is strong - er. God, You are high - er than an -
mp
G/B
Am
F
- y oth - er. Our God is Heal - er, awe - some in pow - er, our God,
1
C
G
our God.
2
C
G
our God.
rit.

REACHING FOR YOU

Words and Music by LINCOLN BREWSTER
and PAUL BALOCHE

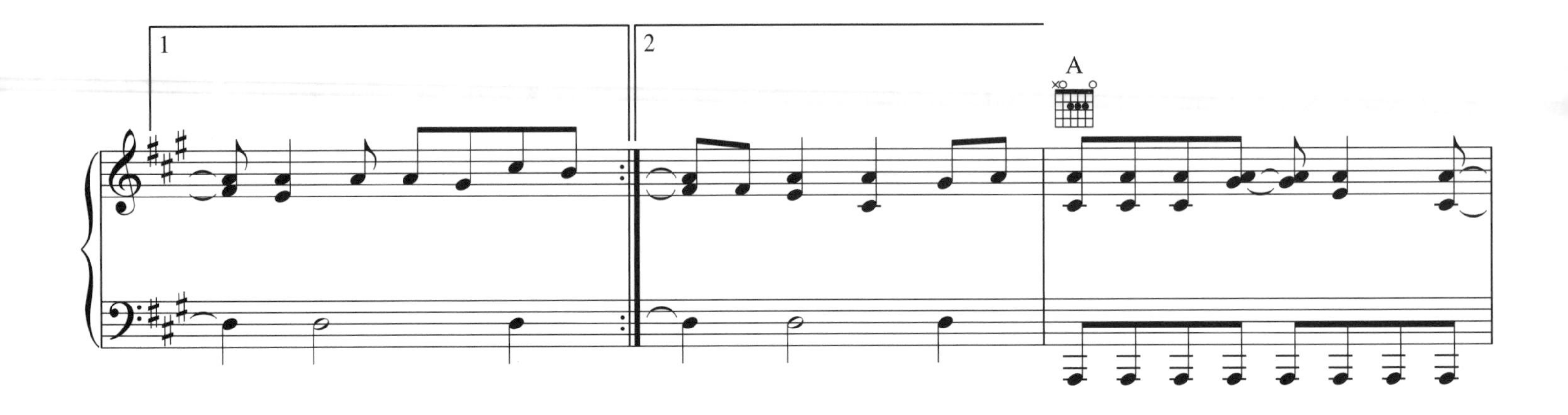

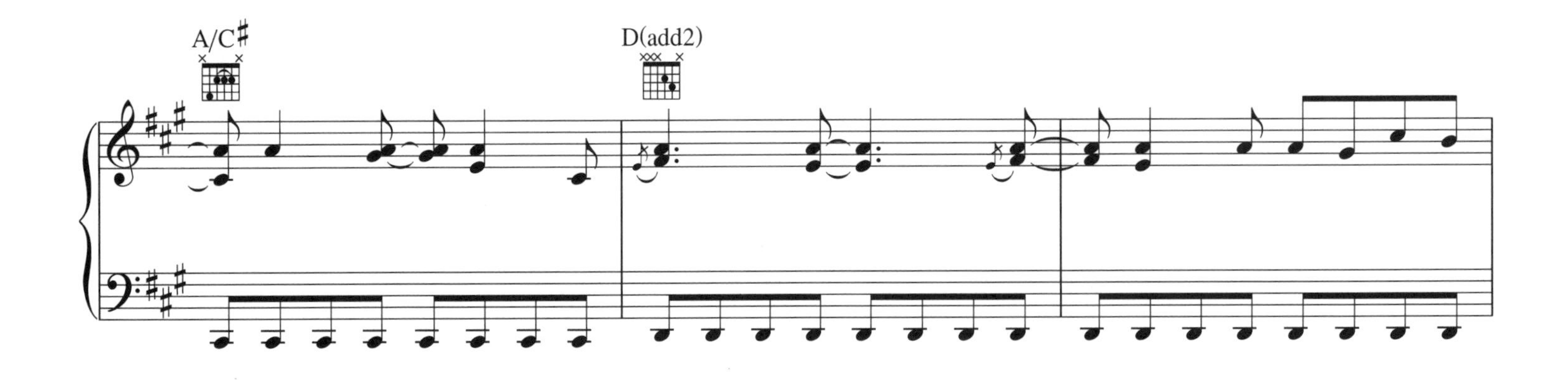

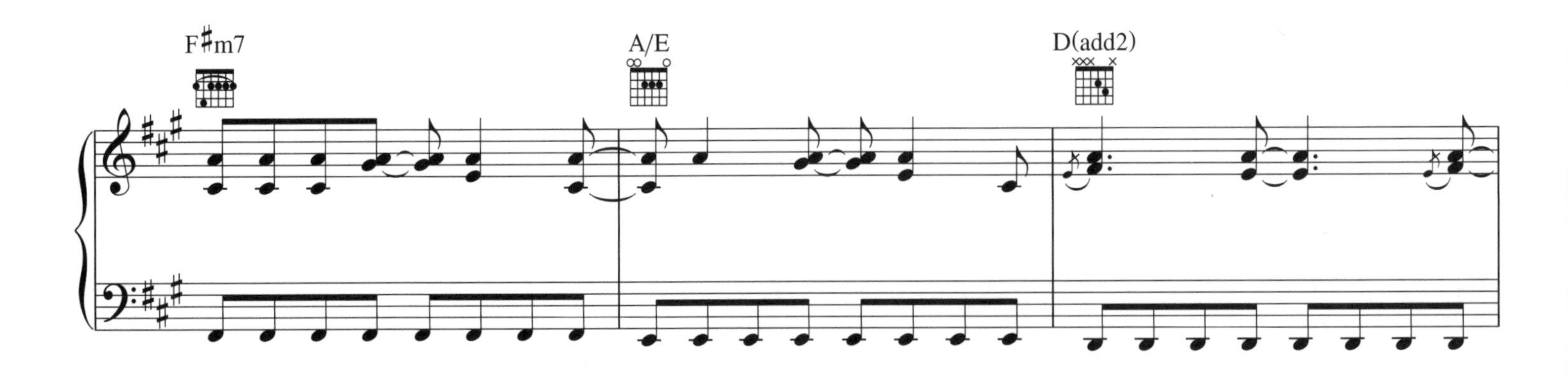

A
A/C♯
mf
You cre - at - ed me in - side Your
D(add2)
F♯m7
great i - mag - i - na - tion.
You're the One who gave
D
me my first breath.
A
A/C♯
D(add2)
You have o - ver - seen my life and brought me to re - demp -

F#m7
- tion, and I know that You're not fin - ished with me
D(add2)
yet.
A
I'm reach - ing for You,
I'm sing - ing to You.
Esus
E
I'm lift - ing my hands
F#m7
to praise You,
I'm lift - ing my voice
D
to thank You.

A
I'm reach - ing for You.
Je - sus, I need
Esus
E
F♯m7
You.
I'm giv - ing my heart to know You,
D
To Coda
I'm liv - ing my life to serve You.
I'm reach - ing for
A
D(add2)
You,
O Lord.

F♯m7
D(add2)
A
You're the One who spoke
mf
A/C♯
D(add2)
the Word of Life to light my dark - ness. You
F♯m7
A/E
D
o - pened up my eyes 'til I could see.

A
A/C♯
Je - sus, You have prom - ised to com - plete
D(add2)
F♯m7
the work You've start - ed,
faith - ful to ful - fill
A/E
D(add2)
D.S. al Coda
Your grace in me.
I'm reach - ing for
CODA
A
I'm reach - ing for You.

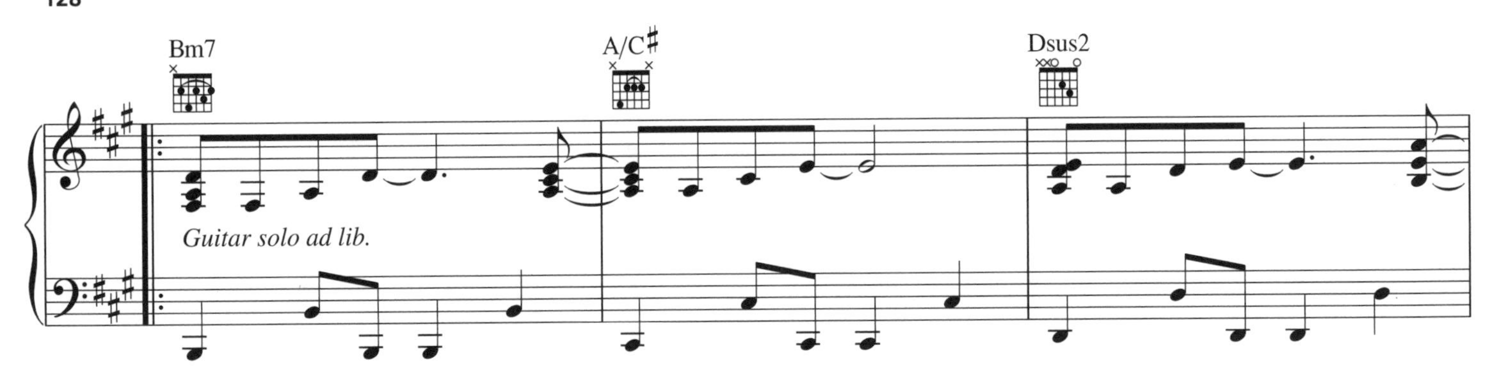
Bm7
A/C♯
Dsus2
Guitar solo ad lib.

Esus
E
Bm7
A/C♯

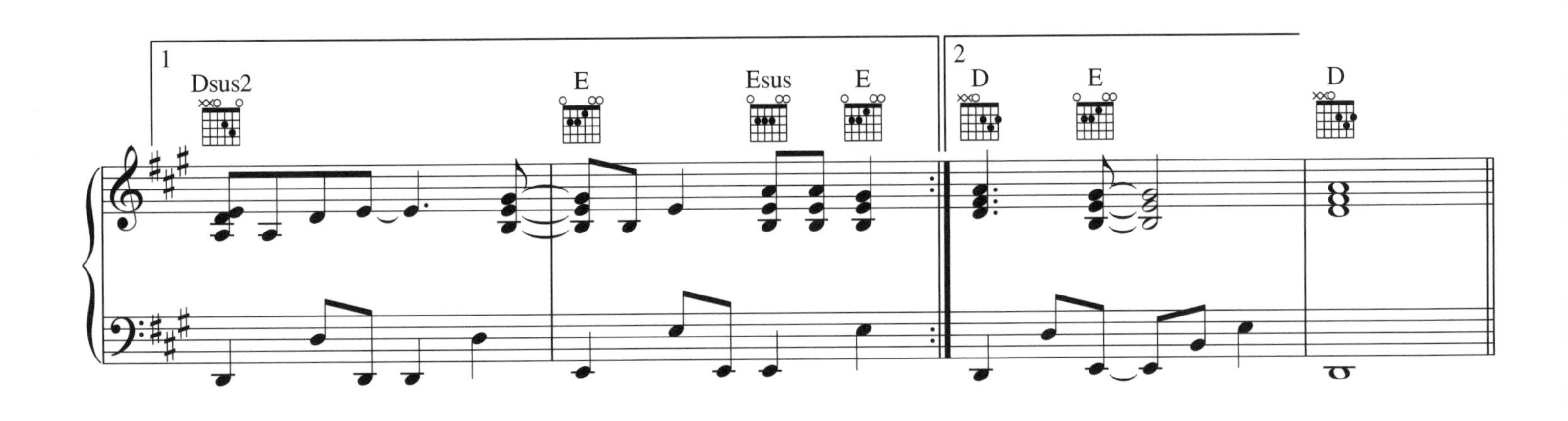
1
Dsus2
E
Esus
E
2
D
E
D

A
E/G♯
Pour out Your love from heav - en, fill me un - til
mf

Bm7
A/C♯
D
I o - ver - flow.
Lord,
'Cause
I want more.
A
Reach down Your hands from heav - en,
E/G♯
Bm7
pull me clos - er than ev - er be - fore.
1
A/C♯
D
Lord, I want more.

2
A/C♯
Dmaj7
Lord, I want more.
I'm reach - ing for
A
Esus
E
A/C♯
You,
I'm sing - ing to You.
I'm lift-ing my hands
F♯m7
D
to praise You,
I'm lift - ing my voice to thank You.
A
I'm reach - ing for You.
Je - sus, I need

Esus
E
Bm7
You.
I'm giv - ing my heart to know You,
A/C♯
D
D/E
D/F♯
D/E
D
I'm liv - ing my life to serve You.
I'm reach - ing for
A
A/C♯
D(add2)
You.
Oh,
F♯m7
A/E
D
I'm reach - ing.
God, I'm reach - ing for You.
rit.

STARRY NIGHT

Words and Music by ED CASH
and CHRIS AUGUST

F
C
from the des - ert sands to the place we stand,
from the paint - ed sky to my plank - filled eye,
Am
G
He is God of all, He is ev - 'ry - thing,
Am
G
C
Whoa, oh. I'm giv - ing my life to the on - ly One who
G
Am
makes the moon re - flect the sun ev - 'ry star - ry night.

F
C
That was His de - sign. I'm giv - ing my life to the on - ly Son who
G
Am
was and is and yet to come. Let the prais - es ring
F
C
'cause He is ev - 'ry - thing,
1
F
C
F
'cause He is ev - 'ry - thing,

2
F
Am
F
ev - 'ry - thing. Hal - le - lu - jah, hal - le - lu - jah,
C
G
Am
I be - lieve, oh, oh. Hal - le - lu - jah,
F
C
G
hal - le - lu - jah, I be - lieve. I'm
C
G
giv - ing my life to the on - ly One who makes the moon re - flect the sun.
mp

Am
F
On that star - ry night,
He changed my life. And I'm
C
G
giv - ing it all to the on - ly Son who gave me hope when I had none.
Am
F
So let the prais - es ring, oh, let the prais - es
I'm
cresc.
C
G
ring.
giv - ing my life to the on - ly One who makes the moon re - flect the sun
mf

Am
F
ev - 'ry star - ry night.
That was His de - sign. And I'm
C
G
giv - ing my life to the on - ly Son who was and is and yet to come.
Am
G/B
And the an - gels sing
that He is heav - en - ly.
C
F
So let the prais - es ring
'cause He is ev - 'ry-thing.

YOUR LOVE

Words and Music by BRANDON HEATH
and JASON INGRAM

Bm
G
D
I tried to sat - is - fy the hun - ger; I nev - er got it right,
Bm
G
D
I nev - er got it right.
3
Bm
G
D
So I climbed a moun - tain, built an al - tar,
You know the ef - fort I have giv - en,
Bm
G
D
looked out as far as I could see.
You know ex - act - ly what it cost.

Bm
G
D
And ev - 'ry day I'm get - ting old - er, I'm run - ning out of dreams,
And though my in - no - cence was tak - en, not ev - 'ry - thing is lost,

Bm
G
D
I'm run - ning out of dreams.
not ev - 'ry - thing is lost.
But Your

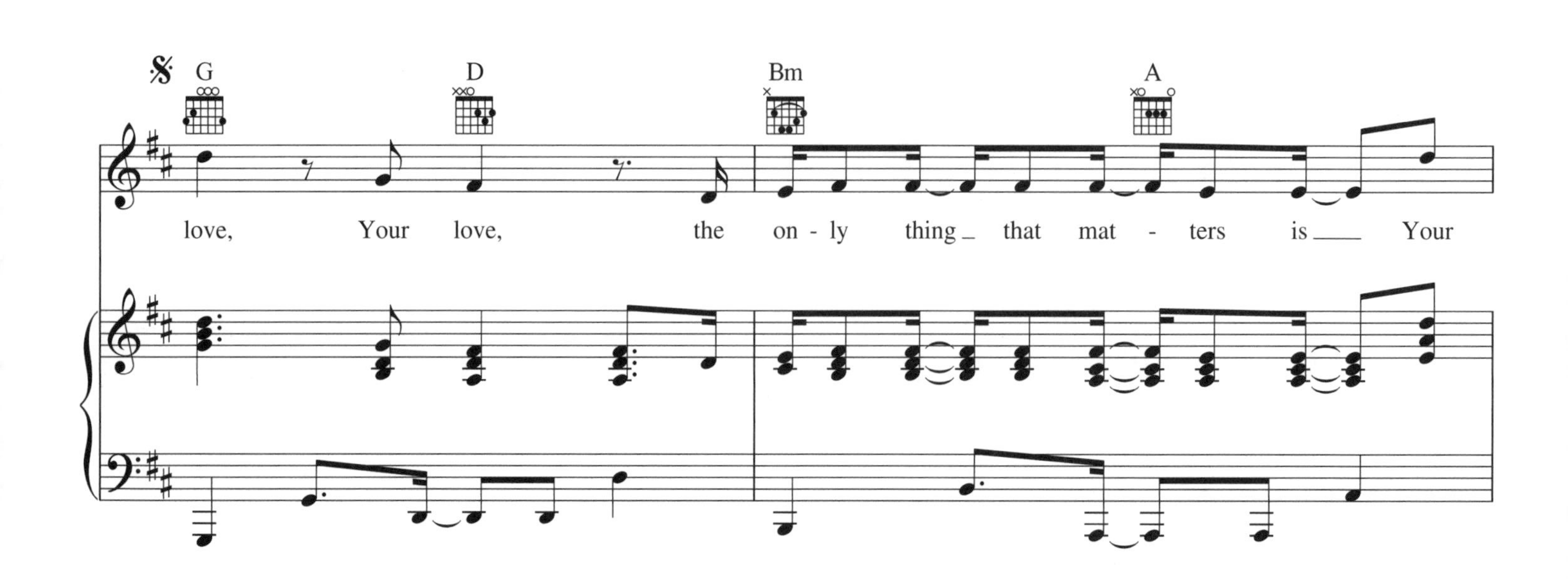
G
D
Bm
A
love, Your love, the on - ly thing that mat - ters is Your

G
D
Bm
A
love. Your love is all I have to give. Your
G
D
Bm
A
love is e - nough to light up the dark - ness. It's Your
G
D
To Coda
1
Bm
A
love, Your love. All I ev - er need - ed is Your love.
Bm
Gmaj7
D

2
Bm
A
G
D
All I ev - er need - ed is Your love.

Bm
A
G
D
You're the hope in the morn - ing,

A
Bm
G
D
You're the light when the night is fall - ing,
You're the song when my heart is sing- ing.

A
Bm
G
D
It's Your love.
You're the eyes to the blind man,
A
Bm
G
D
You're the feet to the lame man walk - ing,
You're the sound of the peo - ple sing - ing.
A
G
D
Bm
A
It's Your love, Your love,
Your
G
D
Bm
A
D.S. al Coda
love.
But Your

CODA
Bm
A
G
D
All I ev - er need - ed is Your love.
Bm
A
G
D
All I ev - er need - ed is Your love, Your love.
Bm
A
1
G
D
All I ev - er need - ed is Your love.
2
G
D
Bm
A
It's all I ev - er need - ed.